This book belongs to

_____

# Impulsive Ninja

### By Mary Nhin

Pictures by
Jelena Stupar

My sister was taking her time with the red crayon. So, I patiently told her...

Whenever I had an impulse to say or do something rash,
I took time to think about what I would say or do next.

When my sister and I were wrestling, I noticed we were doing it in an area where we could possibly knock some things down. So, I paused and asked her to play on the ground instead...

If I was responding to someone, I would take a moment to consider how my words might affect them.

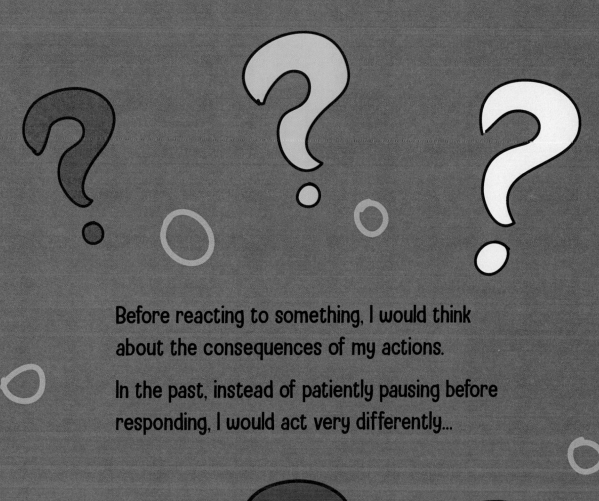

Before reacting to something, I would think about the consequences of my actions.

In the past, instead of patiently pausing before responding, I would act very differently...

For example, when my sister wouldn't give me back my stuff, I screamed on the top of my lungs. I hadn't meant to yell at her, but I was SOOOO MAD!

At school, I struggled with following the rules...

Did inappropriate things for attention...

And had trouble taking turns.

One afternoon while Patient Ninja and I were coding, I got so frustrated that I impulsively punched the screen of my computer.

The next day, I chose to practice my newfound superpower.
And it really made a difference!

At school, even though Jealous Ninja was making me mad with constant pencil tapping, I chose to pause and think about my choices. Instead of shoving or kicking the chair, I politely asked Jealous Ninja to stop.

On the playground, I didn't demand to be the first to have the ball.

Before reacting impulsively, I would consider the consequences of my actions so I could make a better decision.

I really liked how people responded to me when I practiced my superpower of pause. But most of all, I liked how it made me feel great about my decisions.

Remembering to practice your superpower of pause could be your secret weapon in keeping impulsive behaviors at bay.

Please check out our beyond the book
resources at ninjalifehacks.tv

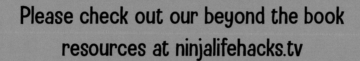 @marynhin   @GrowGrit
#NinjaLifeHacks

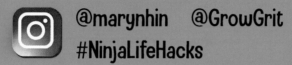 Mary Nhin   Ninja Life Hacks

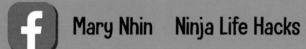 Ninja Life Hacks

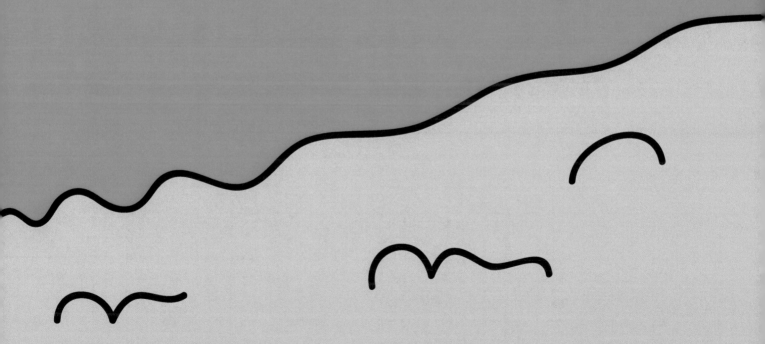

Made in United States
North Haven, CT
07 October 2023